Nigeria

BLAINE WISEMAN

AV² provides enriched content that supplements and complements this book. Weigl's AV² books strive to create inspired learning and engage young minds in a total learning experience.

Your AV² Media Enhanced books come alive with...

Audio
Listen to sections of the book read aloud.

Key Words
Study vocabulary, and complete a matching word activity.

Video
Watch informative video clips.

Quizzes
Test your knowledge.

Go to www.av2books.com, and enter this book's unique code.

Embedded Weblinks
Gain additional information for research.

Slide Show
View images and captions, and prepare a presentation.

BOOK CODE

L588834

Try This!
Complete activities and hands-on experiments.

... and much, much more!

AV² by Weigl brings you media enhanced books that support active learning.

Published by AV² by Weigl
350 5th Avenue, 59th Floor
New York, NY 10118
Websites: www.av2books.com   www.weigl.com

Library of Congress Cataloging-in-Publication Data

Wiseman, Blaine, author.
 Nigeria / Blaine Wiseman.
   pages cm. — (Exploring countries)
 Includes index.
 ISBN 978-1-4896-3058-2 (hard cover : alk. paper) — ISBN 978-1-4896-3059-9 (soft cover : alk. paper) — ISBN 978-1-4896-3060-5 (single user ebook)
 — ISBN 978-1-4896-3061-2 (multi-user ebook)
 1. Nigeria—Juvenile literature. I. Title.
 DT515.22.W57 2014
 966.9—dc23
                        2014038996

Printed in the United States of America in Brainerd, Minnesota
1 2 3 4 5 6 7 8 9 19 18 17 16 15

012015
WEP160115

Project Coordinator Heather Kissock
Art Director Terry Paulhus

Photo Credits
Every reasonable effort has been made to trace ownership and to obtain permission to reprint copyright material. The publishers would be pleased to have any errors or omissions brought to their attention so that they may be corrected in subsequent printings.

Weigl acknowledges Getty Images as its primary image supplier for this title. Page 12 bottom: Wikipedia.

Contents

AV² Book Code 2

Nigeria Overview 4

Exploring Nigeria 6

Land and Climate 8

Plants and Animals 10

Natural Resources 11

Tourism 12

Industry 14

Goods and Services 15

Indigenous Peoples 16

Early Kingdoms 17

The Age of Exploration 18

Population 20

Politics and Government 21

Cultural Groups 22

Arts and Entertainment 24

Sports 26

Mapping Nigeria 28

Quiz Time 30

Key Words 31

Index 31

Log on to www.av2books.com 32

Nigeria Overview

Nigeria is the most populated country on the continent of Africa. Hundreds of languages are spoken throughout the country by people of many different cultural groups. Nigeria's landscape is diverse, as well. It features plains and valleys, **plateaus** and mountains, deserts and wetlands. Nigeria's variety of lands and people make it an exciting country to explore.

Nigeria has large deposits of petroleum, or oil, off its southern coast.

Soccer is the country's most popular sport.

Hundreds of years ago, Nigerians made sculptures of kings and gods.

Nigerians sell produce, such as bananas, at roadside markets.

Drill monkeys can be found in forested areas of southeastern Nigeria.

Exploring
Nigeria

Nigeria covers more than 356,000 square miles (923,000 square kilometers). It is slightly more than twice the size of the U.S. state of California. Located in West Africa, Nigeria borders Cameroon to the east, Chad to the northeast, Niger to the north, and Benin to the west. Its southern border stretches 530 miles (853 kilometers) along the Gulf of Guinea, in the Atlantic Ocean.

Burkina Faso

Benin

Togo

Ghana

Niger River

Gulf of Guinea

N

Atlantic Ocean

Map Legend

 Nigeria

Land

Water

 Niger River

Lake Chad

Niger Delta

Capital City

100 Miles

SCALE

100 Kilometers

Niger River

Nigeria is named after its longest river, the Niger. Flowing a total of 2,600 miles (4,200 km), the Niger is Africa's third-longest river. It begins in Guinea and flows through Mali, Niger, and Benin before reaching Nigeria.

Niger

Chad

Lake Chad

Abuja

📍 *Abuja*

G E R I A

Lake Chad

Cameroon

Niger Delta

*Niger
Delta*

Niger Delta

The Niger **Delta** is a region along the south coast of Nigeria, where the Niger River flows into the Gulf of Guinea. Many different groups have farmed and fished there for centuries. Today, petroleum is the area's main natural resource.

Abuja

Abuja is a planned modern city. In the 1970s, the Nigerian government decided to build a new capital city in the center of the country. Abuja became Nigeria's capital in 1991.

Lake Chad

Lake Chad is Nigeria's largest lake. Parts of the lake are in Niger, Chad, and Cameroon. The lake is shallow, and its area changes as the seasons change between dry and wet.

LAND AND CLIMATE

Nigeria has three main geographical areas. They stretch across the northern, central, and southern parts of the country. In the north, the landscape is mostly **savanna**. The Sokoto Plains of the northwest are lowlands, with some hills rising above them. Toward Lake Chad, the Borno Plains feature areas of ancient sand dunes. The region slopes toward the Lake Chad Basin, which was part of the lake during a wet period thousands of years ago. Most of the basin has dried out.

Only a few types of plants can grow in the Kuri Wakko Dunes of northern Nigeria.

The middle part of Nigeria is a highland region made up of hills and plateaus. The Jos Plateau is an area created by ancient volcanoes. Farther south, several rivers cross the Udi-Nsukka Plateau and empty into the Niger River. The Shebshi and Gotel mountain ranges in the east are the highest points in the country.

Southern Nigeria is marked by lush lowlands and the large Niger Delta region. The delta makes up 12 percent of Nigeria's land area. It covers 43,000 square miles (110,400 sq. km). Near the coast, there are wetlands.

Nigeria has a dry and a rainy season. The rainy season is longest in the south, lasting from March to November. There, the average yearly rainfall is 60 to 100 inches (150 to 250 centimeters). The central part of the country receives between 35 and 55 inches (90 and 140 cm) of rain per year. The north is even drier, with periods of very dry weather called droughts. The average rainfall is 20 inches (50 cm) per year. All of Nigeria has warm weather year-round.

Land and Climate BY THE NUMBERS

About 3,000 Square Miles

Size of the Jos Plateau.
(8,000 sq. km)

95% Amount Lake Chad shrank between 1963 and 2008 because of drought.

Height of Chappal Waddi, the highest mountain in Nigeria.
(2,419 m)

Tropical forests form much of the landscape in southern Nigeria.

PLANTS AND ANIMALS

The diverse landscapes of Nigeria support a wide range of plants and animals. Along the Gulf of Guinea, mangrove forests provide the most common **habitat**. Mangroves are trees or shrubs that grow in coastal swamps or other areas of shallow saltwater. North of the coast, rainforests used to be common. However, large parts of these forests have been destroyed.

In central Nigeria, the grasslands contain trees such as the baobab and tamarind. The drier conditions of the north support only stunted, or very short, trees. In recent times, the Sahara Desert, which covers most of North Africa, has been getting larger. In some areas along Nigeria's northern border, plant life has almost completely disappeared.

In the past, many kinds of animals lived in Nigeria. These included camels, baboons, lions, hyenas, and giraffes in the savanna region. Monkeys, chimpanzees, and elephants were plentiful in the nation's rainforests. Many of these animals either no longer can be found in Nigeria or are very rare.

The forest elephants living in Nigeria have straighter tusks and a slightly darker color than grassland elephants in other parts of Africa.

NATURAL RESOURCES

Two natural resources that are plentiful in Nigeria are fertile soil and petroleum. For thousands of years, people have used the soil to grow crops. Yams, rice, and sorghum feed the local population. Crops such as cacao, which is used to make chocolate, and rubber help Nigerian industries create jobs.

As the population grows, more land is needed for farms. At the same time, **desertification** in the north is reducing the amount of fertile land in that region. Many Nigerians have left their traditional homes to find new land farther south. Farmland is often created by clearing forests. Population growth and desertification are major reasons for the loss of rainforests in southern Nigeria.

The natural resource that brings the most money into Nigeria is oil. Much of the oil produced is sold to other countries. Nigeria has the 10th-largest oil **reserves** in the world. The country also has large reserves of natural gas. Nigeria uses dams on many of its rivers to produce **hydroelectricity**.

1956
Year that oil was first discovered in Nigeria.

2.4 MILLION
Number of barrels of oil produced daily.

9th Nigeria's rank among world nations in natural gas reserves.

Trees cut down from Nigeria's forests are used for lumber.

TOURISM

Tourism is an important part of Nigeria's **economy**. Visitors to the country stay in hotels, take tours, and eat at local restaurants. These activities create jobs and add money to the economy. Nigeria's tourist attractions include natural areas where visitors can hike and view the country's animal life. There are also historic sites and cultural attractions in all parts of the country.

Tourists enjoy visiting the many open-air markets in Lagos.

Lagos, the capital until 1991, is the largest city in Nigeria. Lagos's National Museum opened in 1957. Artworks on display include sculptures and other carved objects from many periods of Nigerian history.

Lagos also features celebrations such as the Eyo Festival. This is a week-long event. During the festival, people from the Yoruba **ethnic group** dance through the streets in traditional clothing.

Stilt-walkers are part of many Eyo Festival parades.

Visitors to the new capital city enjoy its natural and cultural attractions. From almost anywhere in Abuja, tourists can see at least one of two giant rocks. The larger one, Zuma Rock, is 2,460 feet (750 m) tall. Aso Rock stands 1,312 feet (400 m) high. In front of Aso Rock is the Presidential Villa, where Nigeria's president lives.

Cross River National Park was created by the Nigerian government to protect the last Cross River gorillas in the country. The park, on the Nigerian-Cameroon border, contains mountain rainforests where the world's rarest gorilla **species** lives. Cross River gorillas were believed to have become **extinct**, but some were discovered in a remote area in the 1980s. The park built to protect them is also home to 198 other types of **mammals** and 380 bird species.

The Sukur Cultural Landscape provides a view into life in Nigeria hundreds of years ago. A chief's palace built of stone is located on a hill, and several villages lie at the foot of the hill. The city of Jos features a zoo, an art museum, and a museum with exhibits about Nigerian history.

Tourism BY THE NUMBERS

866,000 Number of workers in Nigeria whose jobs involve helping tourists.

$9.8 BILLION
Total number of dollars tourism added to the Nigerian economy in 2013.

200–300
Number of Cross River gorillas living in nature in Cameroon and Nigeria.

Zuma Rock is also called the gateway to Abuja, since it stands on the edge of the city.

INDUSTRY

Nigeria is the 12th-largest oil producer in the world. The country also mines coal, tin, and columbite, which contains iron and other metals. Oil has given Nigeria the largest economy in Africa. However, much of the income from oil sales has not gone to the Nigerian people. Most Nigerians are poor. Many people in the Niger Delta and other regions believe they should benefit more from the country's oil.

Manufacturing is a growing part of Nigeria's economy. Steel and paper mills operate in several cities. Nigeria also has many home-based workshops. Here, people produce pottery, wood carvings, and mats made from the leaves of palm trees.

Factories in Nigeria make products out of rubber or the hides of animals. Cement and other construction materials are produced. Nigerian factories also make food products, footwear, and chemicals.

2.2 Billion Tons
Amount of coal reserves in Nigeria. (2 billion metric tons)

70% Portion of Nigerians who live in poverty.

1903

Year the first rubber plantation, or large farm, was established in Nigeria.

Many energy companies have terminals in the Niger Delta. Oil and gas are stored at the terminals until they are shipped.

GOODS AND SERVICES

About one-fifth of Nigerian workers are employed in service industries. These are industries in which workers provide a service to other people rather than produce goods. Service industries include transportation, health care, and education.

Many Nigerians earn a living from agriculture. Most farmers produce enough food for their families and a little more to sell to others. In recent years, the portion of Nigerians living in cities has increased. The country's farmers no longer grow enough food to feed the population. Nigeria **imports** food from other countries.

Other imported products include machinery, transportation equipment, and many types of manufactured goods. Nigeria buys more goods from China than it does from any other nation. Oil and **refined** petroleum products make up 95 percent of Nigeria's **exports**. Other major exports are rubber and cacao beans. The United States receives 17 percent of Nigerian exports, more than any other country.

About 70 percent of Nigerian workers are farmers.

INDIGENOUS PEOPLES

1928
Year the first Nok culture objects were discovered by miners on the Jos Plateau.

2ND CENTURY AD
Time period when the Nok culture disappeared.

9TH AND 10TH CENTURIES
Period when the Igbo Ukwu bronze objects were created.

Human beings have lived in the area now called Nigeria for thousands of years. **Archaeologists** have found stone tools in Nigeria that are 40,000 years old. Many early peoples hunted animals and gathered plants for food. They may have moved from place to place in search of the best food sources. Over time, some groups began farming and living in the same area year-round.

At least 2,500 years ago, one group built a large culture in the area of the Jos Plateau. Objects made by this group were discovered near the village of Nok, and the group was named the Nok culture. Iron tools, stone axes, and clay figures have been found over hundreds of square miles (sq. km). While their culture began with stone tools, the Nok survived long enough to move from the **Stone Age** to the **Iron Age**.

In the 1930s and 1940s, people in southern Nigeria discovered ancient objects made by the Igbo Ukwu people. These bowls and other items were made of bronze, a mix of copper and tin. They had very detailed and artistic decoration.

Many Igbo Ukwu jars and other objects were made with leaded bronze. Adding a small amount of lead to the other metals made the objects easier to shape and helped them last longer.

EARLY KINGDOMS

For hundreds of years, present-day Nigeria was divided into a number of independent states. Kings ruled many of these states. In the western part of Nigeria, the Yoruba and Edo peoples built powerful kingdoms. By the 11th century, Ife was the main city and capital of the Yoruba kingdom. Then, the Yoruba moved their capital to Oyo. By the 1600s, Oyo and other cities were each small kingdoms. Oyo and the other Yoruba kingdoms declined in the 1800s. South of Ife, the Edo people formed the kingdom of Benin in the 900s.

The Hausa people controlled the northern plains for centuries. The Hausa lived in walled cities, and each city had its own king. Hausa kingdoms fought both with one another and with other cultural groups. The Fulani people conquered the Hausa in the early 1800s.

Not all peoples lived in kingdoms. The Igbo lived in villages. A federation, or group, of villages was led by a council of elders. Igbo women as well as men were members of these councils.

Early Kingdoms BY THE NUMBERS

5,000 Average population of an Igbo village federation.

Late 12th–Early 13th Centuries
Period when many bronze sculptures and other decorated objects were made in Ife.

1650–1750
Years that the Oyo people ruled the area between the Volta and Niger Rivers.

Palaces in Yoruba kingdoms, such as the one at Ikere in southwestern Nigeria, often featured doors with detailed carvings.

THE AGE OF EXPLORATION

For centuries, the kingdoms of Nigeria traded with other cultures. Major **trade routes** went through the territory of the Kanem-Bornu empire around Lake Chad. These routes led to the Nile Valley in Egypt and other parts of North Africa. From there, some Nigerian goods reached Europe, the Middle East, and Asia.

Portuguese ships sailing along Africa's coast first arrived in Nigeria in the late 15ᵗʰ century. The Portuguese began trading with the kingdom of Benin. In exchange for beads, clothing, tools, and weapons, they received ivory and other Nigerian goods. However, what many Portuguese and other European traders most wanted was slaves.

Taken from Nigeria, Olaudah Equiano was a slave in North America and then in Great Britain. He was able to buy his freedom, and he wrote a book about the horrors of slavery.

From the 1500s to the 1700s, European countries took control of most of North and South America. They wanted to use the labor of African slaves in their American **colonies**. Kingdoms throughout southern Nigeria would bring slaves to the ports. There, they were sold to European traders who took the slaves by ship across the Atlantic Ocean to the Americas. As Great Britain became more powerful, it took over much of the African slave trade.

Many slaves from Nigeria were forced to work on large farms or sugar mills in the West Indies.

By the 19th century, many people in Great Britain were against slavery. The British government worked to end the slave trade. It became interested in Nigeria as a source of palm oil and other agricultural products. In 1861, Great Britain took control of Lagos. Over the next 50 years, the British expanded their control throughout the country. Many kingdoms resisted. The Yoruba and Igbo peoples fought wars against Great Britain. However, by 1903, all of Nigeria was under British rule.

Great Britain controlled Nigeria through a system called indirect rule. Local chiefs and other leaders were left in charge of their areas, but these leaders were guided by British officials. The governor-general, who was British, was in charge of the entire colony.

Throughout the first half of the 20th century, the English language and British customs spread across Nigeria. However, many Nigerians did not want to be ruled by another country. They started their own political parties, and in 1960, Nigeria became an independent nation.

The Age of Exploration BY THE NUMBERS

1481 Year that Portuguese traders first visited the kingdom of Benin.

3.5 Million
Number of slaves shipped from Nigeria to the Americas.

1833 Year that Great Britain ended slavery in most of its empire.

On October 1, 2010, Nigerian soldiers marched in a parade to celebrate 50 years of independence.

POPULATION

Nigeria is home to more than 177 million people. It is the eighth most-populated country in the world. While Nigeria's population is already large, it is growing quickly. In 2014, the country's population grew by about 2.5 percent, adding more than 4 million people. About half of Nigerians live in cities and towns, and the other half live in **rural** areas.

More people live in southern Nigeria than in other parts of the country. The south is home to most of Nigeria's large cities, including Lagos, Ibadan, and Port Harcourt. The central region is the least populated. Kano, Nigeria's second-largest city, is in the north.

Although Nigeria's population is high, **life expectancy** in the country is low. For the total population, it is about 53 years. In comparison, life expectancy in the United States is about 80 years.

Population BY THE NUMBERS

About 50%
Portion of all Nigerians who are under 18 years old.

Three-Fifths
Fraction of Nigerians age 15 or older who can read and write.

11.2 Million
Population of the city of Lagos.

Busy streets and heavy traffic are common in Lagos.

POLITICS AND GOVERNMENT

16 Number of judges on the Supreme Court, Nigeria's highest court.

18 Years Old

Age at which Nigerian citizens can vote in elections.

12 Number of states that follow sharia law in northern Nigeria.

After Nigeria gained its independence, conflict between leaders from different regions led to civil war. From 1966 to 1979 and again from 1983 to 1999, Nigeria was ruled by military **dictators**. The current **constitution** was adopted in 1999, and Nigeria has had a more democratic government since that time.

The country's official name is the Federal Republic of Nigeria. It is a republic because its highest leader, the president, is elected by the people. The president is elected for a four-year term and can serve two terms.

The National Assembly has two houses, or parts. They are the Senate, with 109 members, and the House of Representatives, with 360. Both houses must approve a new law. It then must be signed by the president before it can go into effect.

Nigeria has 36 states. In some northern states, where many Muslims live, the people have chosen to follow sharia law. This is a set of religious laws based on the Koran, the sacred book of Muslims.

Boko Haram, a Muslim group in northeastern Nigeria, wants to set up a separate country. In recent years, the group has attacked government buildings, the police, and Christian churches and schools.

CULTURAL GROUPS

Nigeria is one of the most culturally diverse countries in the world. While English is the official language, more than 500 other languages are spoken in Nigeria. The three largest cultural groups are the Hausa-Fulani, the Yoruba, and the Igbo.

Traditional chiefs often wear red, flat-topped hats.

The Hausa and Fulani cultures integrated, or combined, in the 1800s. Today, more than 30 million Hausa-Fulani call Nigeria their home. Some speak the Fulani language, Fula, but most speak Hausa. Arabic and other languages spoken by people of the Sahara have influenced this language over the centuries.

Another Saharan influence on Hausa-Fulani culture is Islam. This is the religion of Muslims. The Hausa-Fulani are known for their ancient palaces and **mosques** in cities such as Kano.

The central mosque in Kano was built between 1460 and 1500.

In southwestern Nigeria, the Yoruba are the major cultural group. The city of Ife, now known is Ile-Ife, is still the central city of Yoruba culture. Most Yoruba men are farmers. The Yoruba are also known as skilled craft workers. Today, most Yoruba are Christians or Muslims, but many still practice traditional beliefs.

In 1967, the Igbo people of southeastern Nigeria tried to break away and form a new country called Biafra. After three years of war, the Igbo failed to gain independence. However, the culture of Nigeria's 20 million Igbo people remains strong. Many Igbo are now Christians, but traditional religious beliefs have also survived. Igbo women take part in both trade and local politics.

ABOUT 20 MILLION
Population of the Yoruba cultural group.

50% Portion of Nigerians who are Muslim.

40% Percentage of Nigerians who are Christian.

AT LEAST 500,000
Number of people believed to have died in the Biafran war.

Dance groups today still perform traditional dances of the Edo people of the kingdom of Benin.

ARTS AND ENTERTAINMENT

King Sunny Ade's musical style features vocal harmonies and complicated guitar work.

The arts have a rich history in Nigeria. The country's cultural mix has led to a wide range of styles and traditions. Early clay and bronze sculptures were known and admired over a large area. Today, Nigerian music, art, literature, and films have spread around the world.

Music and dance are important parts of Nigerian culture. For centuries, music has been used in celebrations, religious practices, and storytelling. The traditional dances of Nigeria are as diverse as the people. Some feature masked dancers and colorful costumes.

In the 1960s, the musician Fela Kuti created a new musical style. Afrobeat combined music from Kuti's Yoruba cultural group with American music. Another popular musician, King Sunny Ade, performs in a style called juju.

The people of Lagos hold a carnival each spring to celebrate their region's rich cultural heritage.

Nigerian writer Wole Soyinka is known for his humor in stories about serious subjects. Plays such as *Kongi's Harvest* and *The Strong Breed* criticize dishonest government. Chinua Achebe wrote about his Igbo culture in novels such as *Things Fall Apart* and *Arrow of God*. Chimamanda Ngozi Adichie has won many awards for her novels. Her books *Half of a Yellow Sun* and *Americanah* have become bestsellers.

The film industry in Nigeria has been growing since the early 1990s. The nickname for the industry is Nollywood, combining the words "Nigeria" and "Hollywood." Nigeria is now the third-largest producer of full-length movies in the world. Movies made in the country are popular with Nigerians because they focus on Nigerian issues.

In 1979, the Nigerian government created the National Council for Arts and Culture. This organization promotes and helps develop Nigerian arts. Lagos's National Library and National Theatre preserve Nigerian arts and help them grow.

2013
Year Chimamanda Ngozi Adichie's novel *Americanah* was published.

500–1,000
Number of films produced each year by Nollywood.

10 Days Average time it takes to produce a Nollywood film.

1986 Year that Wole Soyinka received the Nobel Prize in Literature.

Nigeria's film industry provides jobs for actors, makeup artists, and other workers. Many of the country's films are sold on disks and not shown in theaters.

SPORTS

P eople in all parts of the country play and watch soccer, which Nigerians call football. The national men's team is known as the Super Eagles, and the women's team is the Super Falcons. These teams represent their country in international tournaments.

Both the men's and women's teams compete in the International Federation of Association Football (FIFA) World Cup tournaments. Since 1994, the Super Eagles have played in five out of six men's FIFA World Cup championship tournaments. The Super Falcons have reached the women's World Cup championships all seven times they have been played from 1991 to 2015.

In the sport of dambe, fighters wrap one hand in cloth.

In 1996, the Nigerian men's team won the Olympic gold medal in soccer. Nwankwo Kanu, a member of the medal-winning team, is considered one of Nigeria's greatest soccer players. He scored 13 goals in 86 international matches for Nigeria before retiring from competitive soccer in 2012.

Nwankwo Kanu's teammates carried him off the field when the Nigerian team won the gold medal at the 1996 Olympics in Atlanta, Georgia.

Track and field athlete Blessing Okagbare won a bronze medal, at age 19, in the women's long jump at the 2008 Summer Olympics. In the 2013 World Championships, she took home the silver medal in the long jump and the bronze medal in the 200-meter race. She won several races at the 2014 **Commonwealth Games**.

Traditional fighting sports remain popular. Dambe, a form of boxing, was created by the Hausa people. The Igbo have competed in wrestling since ancient times. Each Igbo village has a wrestling ground. Villages send their top wrestlers to compete against other villages. In each match, the wrestler who lifts his opponent off the ground is the winner.

More Than 6.6 Million
Number of Nigerians playing soccer as part of organized leagues and teams.

15 Age at which Nwankwo Kanu began his professional soccer career.

10.2 SECONDS
Blessing Okagbare's winning time in the 100-meter sprint at the Commonwealth Games in 2014.

At the 2014 Commonwealth Games, Blessing Okagbare won the gold medal in the 200-meter sprint, with a time of 22.25 seconds.

Mapping Nigeria

We use many tools to interpret maps and to understand the locations of features such as cities, states, lakes, and rivers. The map below has many tools to help interpret information on the map of Nigeria.

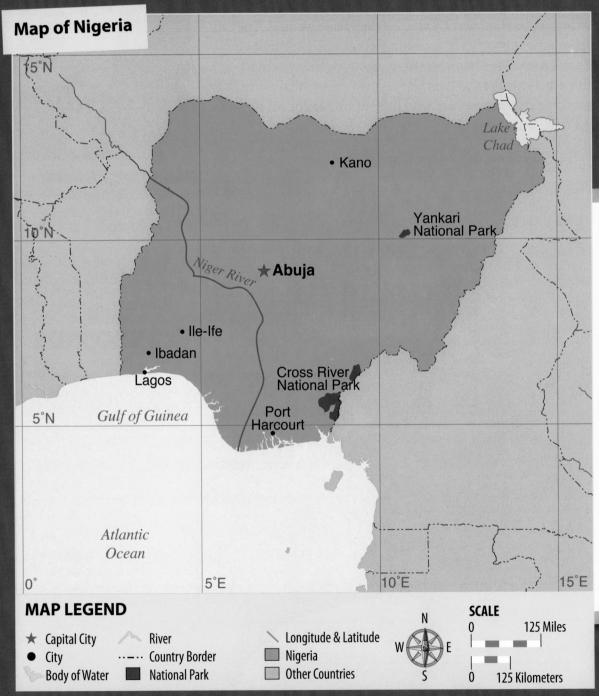

Map of Nigeria

Kano

Lake Chad

Yankari National Park

Niger River

★ **Abuja**

Ile-Ife

Ibadan

Lagos

Cross River National Park

Gulf of Guinea

Port Harcourt

Atlantic Ocean

15°N

10°N

5°N

0°   5°E   10°E   15°E

MAP LEGEND

★ Capital City

● City

Body of Water

River

-·-·- Country Border

National Park

Longitude & Latitude

Nigeria

Other Countries

N W E S

SCALE

0   125 Miles

0   125 Kilometers

Mapping Tools

- The compass rose shows north, south, east, and west. The points in between represent northeast, northwest, southeast, and southwest.
- The map scale shows that the distances on a map represent much longer distances in real life. If you measure the distance between objects on a map, you can use the map scale to calculate the actual distance in miles or kilometers between those two points.
- The lines of latitude and longitude are long lines that appear on maps. The lines of latitude run east to west and measure how far north or south of the equator a place is located. The lines of longitude run north to south and measure how far east or west of the Prime Meridian a place is located. A location on a map can be found by using the two numbers where latitude and longitude meet. This number is called a coordinate and is written using degrees and direction. For example, the city of Abuja would be found at 9°N and 7°E on a map.

Map It!

Using the map and the appropriate tools, complete the activities below.

Locating with latitude and longitude
1. Which body of water is located at 13°N and 13°E?
2. Which national park is located at 10°N and 11°E?
3. Which city is found at 6°N and 3°E?

Distances between points
4. Using the map scale and a ruler, calculate the approximate distance between the cities of Abuja and Kano.
5. What is the approximate width of Nigeria at 10°N latitude?
6. Using the map scale and a ruler, calculate the approximate length of Nigeria's western border.

ANSWERS 1. Lake Chad 2. Yankari National Park 3. Lagos 4. 215 miles (345 km) 5. 550 miles (885 km) 6. 400 miles (643 km)

Quiz Time

Test your knowledge of Nigeria by answering these questions.

1 On which continent is Nigeria located?

2 Which river is Nigeria named for?

3 What percentage of Nigeria's land does the Niger Delta cover?

4 What rare species of gorilla is found in Nigeria?

5 When was oil first discovered in Nigeria?

6 Which country receives more exports from Nigeria than any other?

7 Which ancient Nigerian culture is known for its clay figures?

8 In what year did Nigeria gain its independence from Great Britain?

9 How many states are in Nigeria?

10 Which Nigerian author won the Nobel Prize in Literature?

ANSWERS
1. Africa
2. Niger River
3. 12 percent
4. Cross River gorilla
5. 1956
6. United States
7. Nok culture
8. 1960
9. 36
10. Wole Soyinka

Key Words

archaeologists: scientists who study the cultures of early peoples

colonies: areas or countries that are under the control of another country

Commonwealth Games: events in which athletes from countries that are members of the Commonwealth of Nations compete in various sports

constitution: a written document stating a country's basic principles and laws

delta: an area of low land shaped like a triangle that sometimes forms where a river flows into an ocean

desertification: the process by which an area that used to support more plant life becomes a desert

dictators: leaders who have complete power over their people and who may govern in a cruel or unfair way

economy: the wealth and resources of a country or area

ethnic group: a group of people who share the same cultural background

exports: goods sold to another country

extinct: no longer living on Earth

habitat: the place where a plant or animal normally lives

hydroelectricity: electricity produced using the power of moving water

imports: buys goods from other countries

Iron Age: the period in human history when people began making objects out of iron

life expectancy: the number of years that a person can expect to live

mammals: animals that have hair or fur and that feed mother's milk to their young

mosques: Muslim places of worship

plateaus: areas of land that are higher than the surrounding land

refined: made into a usable product from a raw material, such as petroleum

reserves: the amount of oil available for future use

rural: relating to the countryside

savanna: a large flat area with grass and few trees

species: groups of individuals with common characteristics

Stone Age: the period in human history when people began making tools out of stone

trade routes: the routes commonly used to send goods from one region to another

Index

Abuja 7, 13, 28, 29
Achebe, Chinua 25
Adichie, Chimamanda Ngozi 25
agriculture 15
animals 10, 14, 16
arts 13, 24, 25

Biafra 23

Chappal Waddi 9
climate 8, 9
Cross River National Park 13, 28

economy 12, 13, 14

Fulani 17, 22

Hausa 17, 22, 27

Ife 17, 23, 28
Igbo 16, 17, 19, 22, 23, 25, 27

Jos 9, 12, 13, 16

Kano 20, 22, 28, 29

Lagos 12, 19, 20, 24, 25, 28, 29
Lake Chad 6, 7, 8, 9, 18, 28, 29

manufacturing 14, 15
music 24

Niger Delta 6, 7, 9, 14, 30
Niger River 6, 7, 9, 17, 28, 30

Nok culture 16, 30
Nollywood 25

oil 5, 11, 14, 15, 19, 30

Port Harcourt 20, 28

rainforest 10, 11, 13
religion 21, 22, 23

slavery 18, 19
Soyinka, Wole 25, 30
sports 26, 27

Yankari National Park 10, 28, 29
Yoruba 12, 17, 19, 22, 23, 24

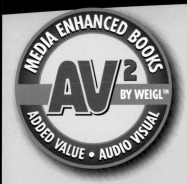

Log on to www.av2books.com

AV² by Weigl brings you media enhanced books that support active learning. Go to www.av2books.com, and enter the special code found on page 2 of this book. You will gain access to enriched and enhanced content that supplements and complements this book. Content includes video, audio, weblinks, quizzes, a slide show, and activities.

AV² Online Navigation

Audio
Listen to sections of the book read aloud.

Book Pages
AV² pages directly correspond to pages in the book.

Video
Watch informative video clips.

Key Words
Study vocabulary, and complete a matching word activity.

Embedded Weblinks
Gain additional information for research.

Try This!
Complete activities and hands-on experiments.

Quizzes
Test your knowledge.

Slide Show
View images and captions, and prepare a presentation.

AV² was built to bridge the gap between print and digital. We encourage you to tell us what you like and what you want to see in the future.

Sign up to be an AV² Ambassador at www.av2books.com/ambassador.

Due to the dynamic nature of the Internet, some of the URLs and activities provided as part of AV² by Weigl may have changed or ceased to exist. AV² by Weigl accepts no responsibility for any such changes. All media enhanced books are regularly monitored to update addresses and sites in a timely manner. Contact AV² by Weigl at 1-866-649-3445 or av2books@weigl.com with any questions, comments, or feedback.